PHOTO GRAPH ING

LOVE

K L KRAMER

authorHOUSE

AuthorHouse™
1663 Liberty Drive
Bloomington, IN 47403
www.authorhouse.com
Phone: 1 (800) 839-8640

© 2015 K. L. Kramer. All rights reserved.

No part of this book may be reproduced, stored in a retrieval system, or transmitted by any means without the written permission of the author.

Published by AuthorHouse 09/24/2015

ISBN: 978-1-4259-8825-8 (sc)
ISBN: 978-1-5462-2006-0 (e)

Print information available on the last page.

Any people depicted in stock imagery provided by Thinkstock are models, and such images are being used for illustrative purposes only.
Certain stock imagery © Thinkstock.

This book is printed on acid-free paper.

Because of the dynamic nature of the Internet, any web addresses or links contained in this book may have changed since publication and may no longer be valid. The views expressed in this work are solely those of the author and do not necessarily reflect the views of the publisher, and the publisher hereby disclaims any responsibility for them.

contents

portfolio
approaching   3
framing lines   4
valentine   5
architect of tongues   6
bill of paradise   7

studios
artistry   11
a hole in my hand   12
grace   13
inchless margins   14
screenplay   15

locations
partners   19
dichotomies   20
transplants   21
surprising em in san francisco   22
postscript (from oahu)   23

shadow icons
the stand-in   27
matinee   28
jimmy douglas   29
jobbing with jane   30
for nancy   32

network
spheres   35
flattery   36
moving targets   37
for john's 30th   38
pathetic   39

wide - angle

and no phoenix rises	43
seeing you yesterday	44
refractions	46
headlines	47
triage	48

mattes

insomnia	51
refinishing (recurring apology)	52
the diver	53
skin-dive	54
esoteric embassy	55

scenario

hospitality	59
trespass	60
cellos	61
primordial	62
spirit	63

split/screen

whose fault	67
divorcing	68
reconvening	69
bitter ends	70
baptism	72

telephoto

simmering	75
opposing mirrors	76
count that high	77
"call me"	78
unchaining	79

portfolio

portfolio

approaching

seizing nuance
dancing cobras
flash markings
each scale a polished facet
a gesture cloaking attitude

isolate moments
pockets of whimsy, discomfort
rack focus to nearest eye
stalagmite irises
freezing thought

or a blur
translucent features
vibrate glass layers
embracing myriad dualities
intimacy pitches

hooded, reactive
we spit at shadows
shed skins
spinal rhythms weaving
through ribbons of dark

Photographing Love

framing lines

the synchronized projectors
popped slides
peruvians on andes
indians in tents
one photographer hung a blanket
to create contrast
conceal clutter

we do steal spirits
from open stances or cornered scrutinies
crow's feet, crooked teeth
generous smiles, glowing skin
we snatch softness, suspicion
pure presence
isn't that the point

fingers roll switches
groping for fabric
speaking images
we all exploit faces
transforming humanity
into boxes
uneasy labels

all of us exploit:
our faces
glistening under the glare
two dimensions before the world

all of us
hang blankets

suck spirits

valentine

     echoes of ten thousand nights
    thread her eyes
     a spider pulling prey

a nature more clever than beauty betrays
               the porcelain exterior
                  beckons
   the world's staccato cacophony and utter clutter
          to remain outside her being

       the altar only seems vacant
  boxes of chocolate so many coffins

                       to we forced outside
       the inner sect remains invisible if not lawless
    cult rituals reduced to tea ceremonies

             generations will not uncover
     our fossilized remnants
  in shared geography

architect of tongues

poised like choice porcelain
your erudite mirages emerge unscathed
simply and sure you speak
calm, offering
mundane pearls:

the acceptance of better possibilities

spirals of jewels
drip polish
vermeer illuminations
irises etched
immaculate, caverns

and you offer only the ideal of tranquility

without expertise
corium
never touching contrast
the texture of aesthetics
the contours of obsession

bill of paradise

pick up the phone
rings continue

unripped envelopes
pile up

you shelve inevitables
with the mail

maybe next month
life will seem less enormous

duplicity won't mean lies
commit won't mean belong

i question obstacles
your love your loathing

is it possession to want
your face daily

to fling our unison
over familial laps

deal now your aces
dreams from the hole

they'll survive
and so will we

studios

artistry

could a painter simply pluck colors from space
to manifest your essence forever on my wall
    or a sculptor endow frigid marble
    with your enigmatic vitality
        or a poet distill from vast vocabularies
        the very words to contain you
            might i feel your pulse
            in the life given creation

            my fingers stroke blue-veined stone
            admiring how jewelers carve facets
        pages polish passion
    when i dream, the pores in your skin wake me
i can never get close enough

a hole in my hand

nothing is as achingly infinite
as the human face

your lips and cheekbones change
in every light

the rush as you turn
suddenly stills

surfaces mesh
cubist composite lingering mid-air

your sinuous glances
probe instantly

sizing, teasing
curving all angles

i reach for your hand
the throne arm waits alone

when you arch limbs over edges
dimensions ray from the chair

even with you folded inside
the corners cannot contain you

grace

        begin in the middle
flurries   of scene and motion
   flux and tension
      absorb   obsessive distraction
        whole days your images fire neurons
   second after second
interrupting
   every hit of thought
               activity
                       i cannot move
             without seeing your limbs stretch
      fragments create their own gestalt
the traces you leave   after the pivot;
  the mood which follows words
       reverbs   from walls doorways
     as you hang in windows

inchless margins

when life sufficiently disembles
we grasp glimmers

too frequently truths metamorphose
word hollows garnish past delays

bubbles of air
break presumption

seeing fallibilities
your textures surface

under my invisible touch
history repeats

studios

screenplay

in the corner a jack waits to catch cold
around this track the hotshots push long poles
our characters play with eyelids and brows
would-bes mingling posh salons and chic crowds
while the stand-in extras help dress the scene
pretense oozes, bit players stage bit dreams
the process tenuous and tedious
either you breed with them and they feed us
or, like the rest, you're only halfway in
endlessly peeling the acetate skin

locations

locations

partners

along the tracks
dust clouds raised
and filled my eyes and arm
through fences
along the clothesline arteries
you have gone to tomorrow
and i to yesterday
one on rails
another on asphalt faith

dichotomies

curled at the bay window
fingertips rap codes
nights stumble against stasis
ready for the warning
when you'll let us know
how well you've failed

driving endless highway
infinitesimal intestines
trying to be there
your contours doze in the hills
snow fireworks flake
fitted sheets

transplants

a hole in the clay pot
seeps dirt
i wait for roots
pushing against
treated soil

weeds gnaw the body
sweaters melt
beyond the sand swirls
pancake stairs
rocky escapes linger

in summer locomotion
fires snake the canyon like a must
fog dissolves twilight
extroverts tonight
our shells leave the bar at closing

on an unlit street our driver sends a kitten
flipping and gasping like a fish
she brakes and another puts out
misery with a brick
the only decision george made all day

hierogylphics of hesitation
etch celestial portraits
moments charge as red lights wink
i wait for the tide
chains of waves

Photographing Love

surprising em in san francisco

stomach spasms spiral
how to survive tonight's full-length ballet
before the midnight flight

three years and you don't even know
we'll be facing tomorrow
despite flu

botulized intestines, vomit
rancid breath
anything for makarova

intermissions i rehearse
while my voyeur friend focuses binoculars
complaining

i no longer have a lemon fix
still tear toenails
still love you and your sister

traffic a beehive drone
i fly the freeways
dreaming of letters

locations

postscript (from oahu)

crystal streams between legs
the wind penetrates our moment
oceans whisper
at each extension of foot or eye
these few hours engrave
implicit photographs

pastoral hills invisible
we blunder japanese cemeteries
night shapes a bamboo epic
the cluttered headstones angle
haunting embrace
full moon branches justify presence

and the darkroom i
mediates and searches for the me
though blinded by the camera
the audience-that-cannot-find-itself
applauds in vain
and in vanity is appreciated

shadow icons

the stand-in

craving billows wings and hotels;
one more night ends with backstage bells.
admirers circle in the midst,
travesty tracks closet exits
searching clubs and hallways for ins.
fate promenades translucent skins
now with no role left to play me
just the contoured absurdity
every lousy direction spat
from aprons chosen to adapt.
parts and lines spell yet more disguise:
you shut out tints; under their eyes
you falter, squint, under the sweat;
we behind drapes place unpaid bets.

matinee

scotch-soaked suede
partners denim
and only washable crepe
times are more than hard
your bets no longer willing
to crash

past cashier windows popcorn counters
hidden lives loom
in the screen version
pride shuns
with cuts only later made
like too many shallow beds

and you wonder
beyond the lobbies of faces
not of our recognition
nor mutual wretchedness
but your limited hours
hands against the wall

shadow icons

jimmy douglas

i listen to your carousel boogie
the honky-tonk of your hollywood
merry-go-round upon round.
those we've met bet success
on each chick they bed
and wed themselves to a roulette
wheel of misfortune.
jim, i turn the tower card for you
thinking of friends who came late.
denim proteges follow arrows
passing piaf to play at your grave.

Photographing Love

jobbing with jane

friends and moms on a first-name basis would ask:
did jane call?
when she did i popped up faster than a boxed clown
showering at a friend's
changing two outfits back and forth
she could give me fifteen minutes

i should have worn the red

at her hollywood hills villa
mattresses margined the sparse living room
my heels rocked wood slats
grilled by third world faces in posters
"war is not healthy for children and other living things"
hung kitty-corner

harsh (pre-klute) ponytail
face adorned only with wirerims
startlingly plain, incredibly dynamic
i in-the-wrong-garb stood
shaking pure dynamite;
in pain, i ceased pumping
she meant to go on

perfectly enunciated
salutations aside, she asked if i spoke french
before i could mention my first semester in college
or, in lieu, anything fractionally witty
the phone rang

she chatted, in french, a fluent fifteen minutes
then hung up, saying she needed to leave
but what a treat it'd been
and her secretary would call

all devastations have a moment of grace
she again phoned personally
en route to paris sans moi

for nancy

at her birth
doctors stabbed adrenalin into her heart
then replaced natural blood with sacs of another letter
a vampire's mere nightcap
filled the tiny, yellow doll

three months later
degreed men addicted
the relentless screamer to barbs
and, over the years, shafted her parents
never themselves, the system, or nature

the asylum teens
offered needles
and jaundiced years
rolled into balls
arteries like yarn

by age twelve
spungen was a bonafide junkie
while i strolled stationery stores
hooked on snapping ink
cartridges into pens

once deceased, immortalized
for whining and cutting and flames
reduced to a celluloid caricature
comedic exaggeration amid
a juliet-inspired pact

network

spheres

journalists jot names and misfortunes
novelists betray secrets
photographers whisk moments
from lapsing dimensions

filmmakers, worst offenders, usurp
your instruments of thought and body
to identify some character;
the actor becomes a communal device

pipelining committee art through the wide-angle.
the public forever taints
your photogenic facades--the gestures, quirks and cadences--
with fiction, rehearsed spontaneity.

despite the linear stories
obvious falsities alter pace;
moving celluloid threads your twists
patterns of pauses
a spherical you immortalizes
with embarrassment and delight:
your youth
your beauty under control

flattery

too long until the gestures confer care
and absorb intimacy
stark fingers crawl frets
dying i wander
groves of cedar neck
lost until this sheet wrestling
reveals with whom i lounge
pitching octaves, horseshoe limbs
sleeping in your bunk
lying with your words

moving targets

cells collapse
cysts sprout
tumbleweed scar tissue the raw silk
patterning gauzed sunlight

threads of foam
on the charging pacific
like saliva crawling craggy skin
as it puffs with each blow

breathing leather
whispery necks interlock
defining gradations
terminal time

we travel with subtle despairs
patched luggage
substituting depots, colors, rolling sagebrush
for percale threads

handles cut palms, i relive your faces
at my hollows like hungry sharks
some gauge syllables
i gouge words liquid hisses

unlit beacons spill light
chugalug sentences like backwoods brandy
fountain verbs and vowels
chilling confusion

the pigeons of wet, recycled spray
regather, distilled
polish the gray edges
like daylight rimming gravestones

for john's 30th

stale effigies
burst from sunburnt pores
as you face another mark

the self-confessed "committed dilettante"
lured your friend to the arcade room;
poised (albeit in a white t-shirt) like rodin's thinker
you contemplated the art in that italian restaurant
as never before

leftover lines from your own blanche
the eurasian before her, the enduring college sweetheart
wind haunting bromides into another day

you smoke metaphysically
a red glow to our pupils
as lungs breathe speechless farewells
your head to a pulsing navel, listening, knowing
nothing is real in the dark

pathetic

the desperate meet the decadent

condom and driver's license, please.
thick palms flip open wallets;
she inspects the evidence.
beneath green glass
smelly shadows sweat smiles.

eyes, iceblue poppies
like futurist tomatoes, stalk.
burnt, they darken
like gooey marshmallows over campfires
falling, dripping.

meccas of distortion invite the nebulous.
watch the dance and ponder
societies, changes.
linking wrists
she faces the door.

wide - angle

wide - angle

and no phoenix rises

the sun would rise
you'd turn and say exist
eyes taunting, inviting sincerity.
hitchhike to ocean middle of night
walk   sleep on beach
i'd be late to class and you to work
if we went at all.

negatives from an old instamatic
hinted how you played to presences
in your room on your bed
fucking best friends;
between us you chose the easier way
betraying everything.
now darkness pervades these lights
my return to this world
welcomed by trivial successes
but rain fills another alley
and i feel you at the window
your face secretly smiling at the anonymous night.

        seeing you yesterday

            dawn
         yawns through slats
              toasting clothes along wooden arms
      i crawl into mine
                   sliding down stairs
                              out doors
   dampness lingers
     wet lanes empty but for a parked car
feet free   i run   until i see you

                  *

           walking a dirt road
        we duck into brush
                      find a stream
    peeling the rhythms of the water
            cuffs rub rocks
  moisture creeps up jeans
        laughter unwinding spirals
                 shoulders sweep trees
                  bark flakes to weeds
   share a leaf
tracing the pattern of its veins
          missing mythical selves
        catharsis tumbles faces
      memories wipe
    each feature rapping some tribal code
              beats finally fade
   as feathers fall

                *

wide - angle

                 there would be hours
    i'd sit on earth   stroking scrolls of eucalyptus
          palming a stone smooth
away from all roads   hidden from relentless noons
not needing to look up this time
              to know you left

refractions

how to define
that part of me which is you

glimpsing moments blurring other moments
like oil slicks melting oblong spectrums
or rust scabbing chrome
the blur becomes reality
just as the moment fades
dissolving in that instant when i need you
grasping dust, i unlearn to not need you

yet where is the reflection now
my cracked mosaic of reality
in which room on what night
might i have found you
on what street in whose bed might i find you
in what mirror
shall i always seek you

wide - angle

headlines

i write my obituaries
author struck by truck
dancer trod by taxi
actor stalked in crosswalk by frenzied fan
after the first successful audition in two years
SURREAL MASK REVEALS OGRE BENEATH

i stroll corridors
jet crashes building
fire breaks out
ESCAPE CLOSED FOR REMODELING:
14 DIE
40 CRITICAL

i prefer preludes to postscripts
things hide in shadows
mailbox throats
i make apathetic comments
then go on
yet i see the newsprint

triage

we breathe battlefields
ducking nuances
like fists
souls on gurneys
wheel past
the wounded
feed the hungry
share the guilt

mattes

insomnia

i drift into watercolors
in the near dark as motorbikes rev
you work your hand shaping the tonal study
somehow seeing what will manifest

a jump: the brush pulls immaculate lines
a lull: a wash laps parchment space
our bodies idle as if charging batteries
unspoken words ripple like your 2-d watercolor pitcher
mimicking bands of light on the model

tablecloth draperies simulate motion
fingers draw life insistent, never simple
turning hues inside-out
sucking us into their eerie, angular deeps

in this stillness senses outline
a world repudiated by our being
in the distance (the next room)
sills and callas invite comparison
colors ooze with their voices

you again blot excess
a grocery bag bloats with toilet paper
while highlighting the vase
you ruined the background

time to remix
adjusting the lamp forearm
you razor patches of epidermis
redraw and blend, creating textures
until the smudged pattern invisibly meshes
i like your skin, your limbs swerve pout
that assuming smirkiness our common denominator
despite this fantasy ghetto
i want to be real with you

refinishing (recurring apology)

nightmares, as splintered tables, need sanding:
smiles perfunctory and clinical
your distance hardly seems the pinnacle
of empathy, humane understanding.
you architect melodramas, planning
how long i'll writhe and wallow; unharnessed
you tease, squeeze, and i swallow; unvarnished
eyes flare verdict, alcatraz expanding.
at first i'd wake, strangled, confused, upset.
you'd throw a switch and verify my gloom;
i focus on your tweed riding outfit
but details, like pores, dissemble and loom:
the intricacies of visions minute--
ideals impossible to execute.

the diver

sunlight blazes golden splinters off her helmet;
the diver glistens in the wetsuit like a seal.
in strangled gestures she shows she knows i'm upset,
that maybe our meeting was postponed by a deal.
fog fills the pier, outboard motors rattle and hiss;
tan figures on a top deck gab over their meal.
climbing aboard, she twists white rope around her wrist,
goggled eyes assessing how despondent i feel.

her silhouette sheds tanks and mask; doubtful but kind,
the shadow summons, embracing although still wet.
a mute fortune-teller, she combs my hand for signs;
eloquently turning gestures like pirouettes
in mime, she pitches a zippered black suit and gear.
with pain-etched brows, the palmist traces shifting lines.
i pose on teak, jumping though the sky grows less clear.
pinched lorelei--too complex for siren divine--
edges over, reading buoys in this chilled mist.
studying charts, eyes catch sparks, oases gleaming.
gold sunlight on the water continues streaming
as the diver again pulls me from the abyss.

skin-dive

snorkeling
in the myths
of your being
whiffs of armpits
reaffirm
my dreamlike presence
plowing navel dust
and you, amphibious, elusive
manage to exist
your head above water

esoteric embassy

the diplomacy of callousness
coils channels
quintessential anxieties
compound cells
tunneling
chess tactics
curtained by art deco
the punch bowl begins
faces crystal cut
unmelting
icicles dangle
free for plucking

scenario

hospitality

hospitality was your ruin

you spoke of asylums
i trampled your threshholds
searching wounds to be nursed

i tailed you to the supermarket
managed to collide shopping carts
amid frozen foods

bought nothing that could not keep

trespass

intruders in fluorescent corridors
affix your silences
failing to transcend

speechless
you cough
fault is prismatically mine

i hammer tacks, splitting the cracks wider
still you're an adult
these passages mutual

my nails are but your teeth
biting your tongue
for unbolting the door

scenario

cellos

bent as if over cellos
branches scrape brutal
wails from the soil

sirens like agonized children
bleed in the circuitry

i sit in the dark, petrified
pulsating spasms shudder

leaves jerk window screens
winds howl like bygone werewolves
sweeping ghosts from the trees

primordial

i am the stillness
beneath all rivers
warming in the earthen core

deep nights swirl
winding private oceans
upon which your sails roll

grains from eroded rock
reflect your pores
ages of pressed palm lines
knot in organs
the abysmal echoes
throughout myriad cells

scenario

spirit

steam films glass
a genie peers
twisting through layers
crouched, bargaining

i offer magic
needing release
needing you
to smash prisons
freeing vapors
disowning command

split/screen

split/screen

whose fault

you rip through repression
a genie erupting from champagne
the bacteria spreads
your eyes teasing light

fungi invade my corpus callosum
mixed messages vaulting
bizarre behavior
like listing sailboats
haphazard destiny
pierces real flesh

a new virus attaches
empathy-empty phone lines
loathing attacks
evanescing my own circuits

divorcing

contorted pauses crawl
frail with desire
extended palms
strive to bridge our exile

baking in unyielding suns
our temperatures rise
from boredom, flesh wrenches
lungs pump, pulse feverish

postulate ifs
explicate the whys
severed snakes
in the mirror

a summer shower
sprays illusion
golden lethargy thickens
ruins glitter

chiselled castles along the aegean
weathered by overstatement, simple logic
labyrinths barren
exhausted

split/screen

reconvening

is this where we file apologies
regret forms for telling pauses
the wrong tone, wrong word, or love mistaken

what court of appeals
would recognize our petty complaints
fundamental as they are

there is nothing to sue for
no fees to collect
only unpaid time

bitter ends

in town the moon hides its aura
asterisk threads from street lamps
prick my head and limbs
a marionette strung by neon
yanked like stigmatizing lines
across my windshield in a prism

glasses exchange mates
after steps of juke rock cruises
the touring blues come survey
lead out handcuffed boys from the backroom
i grip the counter rather than my friend
disgusted yet paranoid and silent

we leave to be scrutinized by the man's
same shade of cronies on the sidewalk outside
proof of existence intact we try again
along licorice lanes headlights hold off the dark
beams strike mirages of puddles
oases in the drought
*

split/screen

riding with tonight's partner
homeward, to where
i'll recognize the streets
i skim the magazine left on the seat
then roll it:
a megaphone for silence

suburbia: camp illustrations
backporches, cars in driveways
conjure and juxtapose
frantic fleeting
pulverized moments
perpetual childhood

a face loops
dancing, he looked fifteen
i remember fifteen
harrowing liaisons
haystack blouses
haze on the windshield

my late stills
flitting, superfluous

baptism

take this steel
puncture these ironclad links
snipped snakes of hair
suspending the coated weight
of all your virginal pressures
strangle those words which close and offend
crush the throat and cram it down the esophagus
knife the neck clean as a lamb
and serve the platter
take this sterling
and weld it with the sweat of your facades
thrust its glimmer into the despairing night
into the tars of futility

telephoto

simmering

mystery shrouds hesitation
malignant conjurings
burst into tempered rods
probing gray crevices

youngsters overturn rock
pursuing swifts
chameleons
uncovering pure vehemence

you light into caverns
fleeing yet beckoning
notorious ritual
shedding victims
dry scales
for fresh skins

opposing mirrors

      we lapse to the zombie zone
      tungsten filament casting charcoal lines
        over deserts of despondency
      my only expectation: no oasis

  side by side we absorb tinted shadows
one pane echoes another ghostly tease
     images of you

count overtures   sizing substance

like flipping over a snapshot and holding it over a bulb
    i ponder how you perceive yourself
  strange how our views of self limit
                           i am the saner for it

        flat gray waves distort our immediate reflections
  in the glare of repeating lights your eyes challenge mine

   shaken
i journey glass labyrinths
    to see how i've held you;
        eventually we'd meet again--we must
is this love-slave devotion or simply love?

        facing off: layers arch eternal
  bending   to infinity
   like miniscule yearnings
     knowing absolute

        yet alone a mirror reflects all but itself

count that high
(anguishing in public restrooms)

confront capillaries
surfacing eruptions between memory darts
domino columns of time period coteries
faction by location
music by liaison

nuanced portraits lace sequences
like traffic clovers
unceasing loops multiply moments when one more word
would perforate
preludes behind wet windshields

eyes race lightlines, connect spots
speckled tiles at feet
the green-purple shadows of stucco ceilings
forearms white as the reflected wall
on-coming blemishes more comforting than the world

visuals harmonize with the whirring fan
flip the switch and time freezes
yet the starkness buzzes
acid afterhours undulating acceptance
of what has or has not passed

"call me"

innocuous phrase jolts from context
a visual flashing mantra embodying temptation
coaxing: servitude
spinning frisbees, neon fantasies;
cycles snowball
an avanlanche of anxiety

i overanalyze yet another awakening
disinterested curiosity now flaming arousal
will i never be too jaded
too burnt

is this rehearsal at keys
much different from the teenager
who kicked walls for three days
awaiting her best friend's call

friday i probed my last best friend
about divorce
all through the concert
a mandala rotated
tendering dangerous ideals
a succubus after substance

unchaining

angles link as speakers pound, lips close
figments mesh, playing "telephone" against the blare
we could slip notes while dancing
"you make me feel like warm gelatin"
contouring bodies for witnesses

drink volumes with the best
the worst under tables, cigarettes curled in fists
smoky phantoms swirl; slippery glasses ring surfaces:
a sabbatical of sexy skirmishes
easy enough, but should you wish to examine us

confront the tomes of dank agonies, dry betrayals
the late edition is yours
cuddle in a corner
with that thread of domino reactions, me,
consider those personae you destroyed

and i'd confess pages
outrageous slights and the slightly outrageous
share your monster
and i'll bare the beast
bathetic and unchanged